Connections

When the evening comes
from the rice leaves at my gate
gentle knocks are heard
and, into my round rush hut,
Autumn's roaming breeze makes its way.

~Dainagon Tsunenobu (11th century)
translstor, Clay MacCauley

Connections

Morning Dew: Tanka
Larry Smith

core & all: haiku
Barbara Sabol

Laughing Buddha Series
Bird Dog Publishing
Huron, Ohio

Copyright © 2022
Barbara Sabol and Larry Smith and
Bottom Dog Press/ Bird Dog Publishing
PO Box 425 / Huron, OH 44839
Lsmithdog@aol.com
http://smithdocs.net
ISBN 978-1-947504-36-3

Credits
Editors: Barbara Sabol & Lary Smith
Cover art: a cairn on the beach (Shutterstock)
Art on Morning Dew by Larry Smith
Art on Core & All: Zen Stone Balance
(Shutterstock)
Cover design: Susanna Sharp Schwacke

Morning Dew
Tanka

Morning dew
speaks, Welcome. Welcome.
All is for your healing.

Tender it licks your feet.
Sunlight in drops

Larry Smith

I rise up early
and feed my waiting dog,
release her to the yard.

A new sun rises through trees.
Wet grass kisses my feet.

Lying in bed
my thoughts from a journal
vanish with the moon.

The wood thrush builds
but a single nest.

Fly at my lamplight
starting the day with a buzz.
Am I any better?

My shoes by the front door
waiting to be filled and tied.

A crescent moon lingers
over a dark ban of trees
water running over rocks.

In morning light we set out,
back and legs tasting pain.

Far off a long train whistle
reminds me of my mother
gone now thirty years.

Wind outside my window
whispers and sighs.

The road narrows up ahead;
bike's wheels rumbling at road edge.
Too long without a drink.

My vision blurs with sweat.
May the sun set soon.

    *   *   *

    Asphalt turns to gravel to earth,
     forcing my pedals to chase
    my breath grown stronger.

    Smell of wet grass and mushrooms
    beneath the trees.

    *   *   *

Biking back from woods
beside the hot asphalt road,
two bird cages nest.

Under a field of clouds,
a train whistle howls.

On the road to Columbus
sunlight warms bright fields
of corn, soy, alfalfa.

Old tunes on car radio
hold each moment longer.

On Anthony Bourdain
"Tony was always running after something,
even when there was nothing to run after."
~Josh Homme

Cycling along the road edge
weeds of purple and yellow
call out my name.

When I get to trail end,
I turn right around. Why?

The bright Cardinal
lands in bird seed, scaring
the golden finch away.

Young lettuce thin as paper
grows taller every day.

A blue jay sits on Buddha's head;
another feeds on scattered seed in grass.
Thoreau would have journaled this:

"Ohio blue jay arrive from the South
hungry for food and meditation."

From the sweet dark earth
cicada wake to their labor,
leaving children behind.

Their message in their song
of sayonara.

A grackle parades herself
around the feet of our St. Francis
shameless in her strutting.

The morning sun rises
and falls on us all.

Great blue heron
standing like a King
stares into water,

lily pads floating
at his feet.

The gray seagull struts
down the fisherman's pier:
"Catching anything?"

Out on choppy waters
boats circle near the lighthouse.

A line of sparrows
along the railroad track—
trusting vibrations.

Two girls scurry across
breathing hard and quick.

In golden light
white egret perch in trees
along the riverbank.

Scent of pine and grass
silence between us.

Under the willow tree,
I read the ancient poets, watch
incense trails caress the leaves.

Sun and shadows through deep woods,
cool spring water.

The wind through pines
wakes a wood thrush
to morning song

Yesterday's losses
today's gains.

Thin blades of grass
press the vinyl fence,
where last year's pinecones

burrow into the earth
smelling of sweet spring.

   * * *

Sun rising through trees
as my fingers become tools
for pulling weeds

so lush yet tight
to the ground.

Along the Monongahela
down from Westover Bridge
wind whistles through willows.

And fishermen in early spring
cast thin lines of hope.

Letting

"Sitting alone I keep slipping away."
                    ~Han-Shan

Below soft clouds
wild geese in gray sky
call out directions.

Incense burns itself out
in scented trails of smoke

   * * *

Train whistle at noonday,
the dog whines and runs
through his dreams,

and I sit here measuring
my life in breaths.

Thoughts and feelings slide
through curtain lace as sun
warms the room with light.

Counting breaths, I float,
dog snoring at my feet.

On sunny days I walk
a trail through woods,
become the things I see,

drink cool spring water
from an old tin cup.

a circle of friends
chant on hardwood floors
at the yoga studio.

out the window on a branch
a warbler echoes their song.

Outside the yoga windows
telephone lines slant
in morning rain.

Inside the room
chanters connecting.

Not what we see but how.
Not taking or making images,
but receiving them whole.

Being the tree we see—
each blossom, each leaf.

That stillness that comes
like a river touching everything
and everyone with kindness.

Every flower, each leaf
the song of silence again.

At Home I

Mother throws our shoes
off the back landing
to sleep in the yard.

The shoes wake in wet grass
our lost children.

Brother picks pimples
at the bathroom mirror,
closes door and locks.

My jeans where I dropped them
asleep on the floor.

The dog stands ready
to lick clean
his wooden bowl.

Father pours tea
into his once shiny thermos.

At Home II

Two eggs wet and warm
naked on the plate—
my dream girl.

Smell of bacon cooking
erases all thoughts.

Slow but sure
we move about the kitchen
without any words.

Sister standing on the register
in her Indian blanket.

Sweetness

Above a steady strumming
a melody rises—
water over rocks.

And your clear soft voice
breaks my heart remembering.

* * *

When we make love
we are nineteen again
kissing what's still there.

Bamboo in snow or sun
bends without breaking.

Out Dining

Sitting at the corner table
above the Vermilion River
we laugh at the boat names.

Ann drinks an iced Lube-a-rita,
I, a tall Blue Moon.

Lying in warm bath waters
I am walking into the Ganges.
Flowers and filth floating round me.

In bright daylight I bathe with them,
brown faces reflecting off my white.

Sounds of wind
inside my CPAP mask...
ocean in a shell.

Grandparents brought back coral
hard and already dead.

A friend not seen for a long time
follows a lone path into his
wilderness of fear and doubt.

South winds over a forked road
blow across a silent lake.

      * * *

An old farmer
walks into the woods alone
and finds in the old pump house

a burry of rabbits nestled
where dogs can't find them.

Placing each stone
beside the bench where
dead friends once sat.

Wild geese overhead
echo their names.

The poet's ashes
float on the river he loved
then slowly sink.

His words stay to embrace
the wind, the sun, and rain.

(for Tim Russell)

The Tanka: Author's Statement

In 5 lines, 31 syllables, more or less, it captures a sensory world that is spiritually alive. One of the oldest Chinese-Japanese poetry forms, originally used in letter writing, like its sibling haiku form, it has long been associated with Zen Buddhism.

Much adapted in many languages today, its conciseness brings a refreshing directness and subtlety to our writing. Unrhymed yet never flat, its intuitive turnings and links, especially between stanzas, empower its brevity through suggestion. The tanka is a refreshing cup of awakening to ourselves and the world sharing its diversity and commonality.

A sample from Taigu Ryokan (1758-1831)*
Visiting Old Mr. Chiku Kyu #1

I know I can't forget my old friend.
So, I knock on the door of his country home
and hang my walking stick there.

Among misty green woods,
a bright bloom of red peony.

Another sample by Michael McClintock (2020)

One bird
on a fence post
singing with all its might

Is all it takes, and the mountains
will all turn green

Acknowledgments

I thank my fellow writers at the Firelands Writing Center for their continued advice and support. Also, I thank Allen Frost, Mike James, Clarissa Jakobsons, Kurt Landefeld, and of course my family: my wife Ann, son Brian, and daughters Laura and Suzanne, and all my grandkids. They keep me going. Special thanks to my haiku writing colleague Barbara Sabol for her inspiration and good spirit.

In a larger sense, I am indebted to all the fine Asian poets of old and the many contemporary poets who shared their lives and visions through verse. They achieve a kind of sincerity that transcends and transforms. Always I am indebted to the journal writings of Henry David Thoreau, so close and dear.

Some of these poems have appeared in the following publications: *Zen Poetry, Modern Haiku, As It Ought to Be, 44839 Anthology*, and others. Some poems appeared previously in *Each Moment All* (Bird Dog Publishing, 2012).

*The Ryokan tanka is a translation by Larry Smith and Mei Hui Huang.

Larry Smith grew up along the Ohio River in the steel mill town of Mingo Junction. He worked as a newspaper boy, cook, steel mill worker, then taught high school in Euclid, Ohio. His education came from Muskingum College, then Kent State University. For 35 years he taught writing and film at the Firelands College of Bowling Green State University in Huron, Ohio, where he and his wife Ann, a nursing professor, raised three children.

He is the author of 8 previous books of poetry, 5 books of fiction, 2 literary biographies, 2 books of Chinese Zen poetry translation. He wrote and co-produced documentary films on authors James Wright, and Kenneth Patchen. With David Shevin he co-founded Bottom Dog Press in 1985 and has edited and published 216 books of fiction, poetry, and memoir. He has directed the Firelands Writing Center for 40 years. In 1980-1981 the Smith family lived in Sicily where he taught literature as a Fulbright Lecturer. Together with Ray McNiece they edited the *America Zen: A Gathering of Poets* nthology in 2004.

In 1990 Smith studied haiku and tanka with Clark Strand at Mount Tremper Zen Monastery near Woodstock, NY. He is a member of the Tanka Society of America, and fond on cycling and playing guitar.

core & all
haiku and senryu

Barbara Sabol

*We take them out of our breasts
and hold them out to each other,
the glass hearts, the transparent bodies.*
           ~Ruth Stone

biscuits & jam

the bellbird
spreads her wings—
aubade

singing bowl
the lullaby's
round notes

lambing
clouds deliver
new snow

chased
by her own wake
water strider

moon and i cross the night pond

surfacing
under a new moon
water tiger

plastic milk jug
filled with spent batteries...
the new mom nods off

nightlight
discovering
her shadow

ballet class
her bat pose
at the bar

porcelain tea set—
forgetting to pour
for the imaginary friend

swimming in the great lake sturgeon moon

orb weaver—
even the spider
centered in space

biscuits & jam
her sticky hand
in mine

never far
from home
garden snail

cocooned still dreaming of flight

                                    cloud cover
                                    hollowing into the bole
                                    in Pop's old oak

unwinching
the porch swing
spring equinox

wishes
unfulfilled
the mown lawn

blood moon
the rabbit's ear
pinker

                                        penny candy
                                        she tries on
                                        the edible lipstick

aces in the spokes

the heady scent
of printer's ink—
first day of school

home room bell—
the garden Buddha's
raised right hand

planetarium
in search of
a safer world

homesick
gazing at Day Glo stars
above my bed

coasting downhill
   aces
      in
         the
            spokes
               syncopate
                  summer

grinning
among the petunias
a stone gargoyle

street light curfew
how the neighbors learned
my middle name

river-smoothed
       skip
              ping
                    stone
un smooths the river

mill town
somewhere in the sooty sky
stars
                    stars
     stars

                                        appalachia
                                        the abandoned quarry
                                        our riviera

picture window—
the view beyond
hogback ridges

autumn blaze
this fire
in my belly

smoke screen

smoked paprika
our hotel dinner
barely touched

burrowing fiddler crabs
we walk the beach
without speaking

summer thunder
whole body shudder
just after

nocturne—
the nightjar calls
from the jar of night

moon flower
the night garden
fragrant with light

mom's green thumb...
the cabbage moth's daily visits
to my garden

elusive fluting deep within the wood, thrush

chiaroscuro
sparrows shake
the shadow branches

seedpod rattle
missing the daughter
I never had

cloud tear
dragonflies multiply
over the pond

glass lake
trailing my fingers
through the clouds

far-off ice floe a mute swan raises her head

doll house
where my real family
still lives

smoke screen
stories we tell
around the fire

morning headlines
my coffee turns
bitter

first frost the finch's visible song

star gazing
the folded flag
in her lap

                        among the junk drawer clutter
                        dad's dog tags

sugar undissolved
at the bottom of my cup—
last day at the cabin

rush hour
daydreams interrupted
by potholes

sunrise...
coyote gathers
his shadow

covering my bases—
    prayer flag draped
        around the crucifix

silk reeling

that turned-down smile
men now give me—
middle age

motion sensor lights the path the wolf once walked

surprise bloom
in the gooseberry bramble
late love

night-blooming cereus...
I whisper my secrets
while you sleep

swash and ebb
of the moonlit beach—
 pillow talk

simple life
the vase content
without flowers

the world news
i eat my apple
core and all

spindrift
losing myself
in the waves

baggage claim
an older woman
reaches for my case

                                               anonymity
                                               tinted windows
                                               of the Greyhound

community garden
so many names
for lettuce

my grumpy neighbor
smiles
cactus blossom

fresh-cut grass
the kid in me
steps to the plate

covid summer—
weeds knee-deep
in the ball field

glacial lake
the stories
I'll never know

forgiveness
the gingko's leaves fall
all at once

another shooting
leaves of my prayer plant
unfurl

sunset over the marsh
roseate spoonbills draw down
the sky

gilded steel rail
the alchemy
of October light

her letters
all these years later
pinkie swear

leaves catch
in the garden rake—
estate sale

waning days...
geese call a vee
in the evening sky

evergreens hold
the old snow's weight
New Year's Day

silk reeling...
rain returns
as mist

perfectly seasoned
cabbage soup
mom's wooden spoon

adjusting
the rearview—
moving day

immense heaven

code status
crows align
on the wire

cemetery walk
I lift my face
to the rain

introspection...
sunfish circle
the egret's reflection

beginning to heal one mourning dove calls

meeting myself
deep in the woods
twin leaf blossom

last blue blaze—
tread worn thin
on these old boots

atop the tomb
a bird I can't identify
the unknown soldier

candles dipped
deeper still
winter solstice

reflecting telescope—
squinting
into the past

open house
empty snail shell
in the garden

passing the oolong
our fingers touch
leaf flush

the way she turns the earth cloud hands

dad's map
of the European theater
tissue-thin

the corner beggar
his blue eyes
like my father's

morning meditation
keeping the prickly lettuce
in check

as if I could have found all the answers the empty bowl

immense heaven
feeling the tug
of other galaxies

late epiphany—
replacing the porch light
in the dark

imago—
no longer dreaming
of flying

red tail and i ride the cloudless blue thermals

The Haiku: Author's Statement

The short-form poem is a kind of lens: the haiku brings into precise focus the natural world, the senryu more the world of human interaction and events. Writing haiku has honed my attention and prompted me to pause and look at the world more closely.

Haiku is a pared lyric nugget usually composed of two parts: a fragment and associated phrase. The poem captures the kind of moment that wakes our senses, our spirit, our intellect, but not always in words. Ideally, it gives that moment words, yet at the same time leaves the sense of something ineffable, something yet to be named or discovered.

In line with the English Language Haiku (ELH) convention, what matters is not syllable count and number of lines. My intention is to ground the short-form poem in concise, direct language, musicality, and concrete, sensory imagery. The core of the poem is the tangible image. The lens zooms in on a subject—some element of nature or human behavior—for a close view, then moves to focus on a comparative or contrasting image. The aim is a perceptual shift from one part of the poem to the other: a juxtaposition of fragment and phrase. If that shift engenders surprise or a new awareness, for both the poet and the reader, the poem has done its best work.

~Barbara Sabol

Acknowledgments

I am indebted to the wide community of haiku friends, most especially those from the Ohio Haiku group, who have helped foster my practice of the short form poem through instruction, feedback, and support. Enormous gratitude to Larry Smith of Bird Dog Publishing for his belief in this book, and for the great pleasure of sharing the pages of this dual collection with him.

Deep gratitude to the editors of the following journals, in which these poems were originally published:
Acorn; Akitsu Quarterly; Autumn Moon Haiku; Blōō Outlier; Bottle Rockets; Brass Bell; Cattails; Failed Haiku; Frogpond; Haiku Dialogue; Kingfisher; Modern Haiku; Neverending Story; Pages Literary Journal; Presence; Prune Juice Journal; Seashores; Stardust; The Heron's Nest; Tiny Words; tsuri-dōrō; Under the Bashō; Whiptail Journal

Gratitude also to the editors of the following anthologies where some of these poems first found a home:
Haiku North America '21 Anthology, Michael Dylan Welch, ed.
Haiku Society of America Members' Anthology, Jay Friedenberg, ed.
Behind the mask: haiku in the time of covid-19, Margaret Dornaus, ed.

Barbara Sabol was raised in Pennsylvania coal and steel country, a place that has strongly inspired her writing. After working as a waitress, barber, and secretary, she attended the University of Massachusetts and began a long career as a speech therapist. Barbara's been writing poetry for more than 20 years, and holds an MFA from Spalding University.

She is the author of four collections, most recently *Imagine a Town* which won the 2019 Poetry Manuscript Prize from Sheila-Na-Gig Editions. She has since taken on the role of associate editor of Sheila-Na-Gig online.

Barbara conducts poetry workshops for Lit Cleveland, and enjoys guest teaching poetry classes at Our Lady of the Elms High School in Akron, Ohio. When she's not writing, Barbara's in her garden or on a trail in the Cuyahoga Valley. She lives in Akron, Ohio with her husband and two wonder dogs.

LAUGHING BUDDHA SERIES

Connections
Morning Dew: Tanka Larry Smith
and *core & all: haiku* Barbara Sabol
America Zen: A Gathering of Poets
Editors Ray McNiece & Larry Smith
The Records of Kosho the Toad
Robert Tremmel
Each Moment All
Larry Smith
Tu Fu Comes to America
Larry Smith
The Kanshi Poems of Taigu Ryokan
Trans. Mei Hui Huang & Larry Smith
Songs of the Woodcutter: Zen Poems of Wang Wei & Ryokan
vocals, Larry Smith, flute Monty Page
Chinese Zen Poems
Trans. Mei Hui Huang & Larry Smith

Bird Dog Publishing
http://smithdocs.net

www.ingramcontent.com/pod-product-compliance
Lightning Source LLC
Chambersburg PA
CBHW021016090426
42738CB00007B/808